THE COLORS OF MANKIND

THE COLORS
OF MANKIND
The Range and Role of
Human Pigmentation

By

SPENCER L. ROGERS, PH.D.

Research Anthropologist
San Diego Museum of Man
San Diego, California

Professor of Anthropology, Emeritus
San Diego State University

CHARLES C THOMAS • PUBLISHER
Springfield • Illinois • U.S.A.

Published and Distributed Throughout the World by

CHARLES C THOMAS • PUBLISHER
2600 South First Street
Springfield, Illinois 62794-9265

© *1990 by* CHARLES C THOMAS • PUBLISHER

ISBN 0-398-05643-9

Library of Congress Catalog Card Number: 89-20390

Printed in the United States of America
SC-R-3

Library of Congress Cataloging-in-Publication Data

Rogers, Spencer Lee, 1905-
  The colors of mankind : the range and role of human pigmentation /
by Spencer L. Rogers.
      p.   cm.
  Includes bibliographical references.
  ISBN 0-398-05643-9
  1. Color of man.   I. Title.
  [DNLM: 1. Evolution. 2. Skin Pigmentation.   WR 102 R729c]
GN197.R64   1990
573'.5—dc20
DNLM/DLC
for Library of Congress   89-20390
                                                                           CIP

ACKNOWLEDGMENTS

I wish to acknowledge most sincerely the help given me in bibliographic matters by Jane Bentley, Librarian of the San Diego Museum of Man. Her assistance has been invaluable.

I wish also to express thanks to my wife, Helen, who performed a most useful service in extirpating the rhetorical and orthographic gaffes that infect the atmosphere wherever manuscripts are in preparation.

Again I express gratitude to Patricia Burton, who typed the manuscript. Her ability to decode my hierographic script and esoteric symbols is remarkable.

Spencer L. Rogers

CONTENTS

THE COLORS OF MANKIND

Chapter 1

THE RANGE AND RECORDING
OF HUMAN PIGMENTATION

INTRODUCTION

The most significant part of the environment of human beings consists of other human beings. We go through life meeting, recognizing, and greeting other persons. For each individual we encounter, this starts with a visual impression of the person's body in its most characteristic details, which includes body size and proportions, and the color of his skin, hair, and eyes. These details of pigmentation are often more consequential than any other physical variable in human appearance: they form a part of an image involved with race, family, and individual identity. In the following discussion we are concerned with the characteristics of color that form part of this image.

The colors of the human body are the result of a complex biochemical process that is but partially understood. These colors frequently lead to acceptance and trust or to suspicion and rejection. They may promote sexual attraction or disinterest. They are a vital part of the mechanism of human interaction that energizes human society. Our task in this work is briefly to examine the physiology of pigmentation in the human body and to review some of the major theories as to the significance of body colors in human evolution.

When human beings first emerged from their infrahuman status they found themselves surrounded by many kinds of animals. Some were basically like themselves, but different in certain details. Others were of varying sizes, shapes, and colors. It became important for these many kinds of creatures to be recognized in some type of classification. Some were dangerous enemies, others were desirable as sources of food or industrial materials such as bone, hides, leather, horns, and teeth. Others were helpful for companionship and protection. The primary details useful in recognizing these creatures were size, shape, hairiness or hairlessness, and color. These same criteria were important in recognizing

3

other humans as well as lower animals. The color of humans and that of other animals was well seen in the skin, hair, and eyes. In some animals color was in splotches, spots, stripes, and all over shades. In humans color mainly occurred in all over shades, but occasionally in spots that we know as freckles, birthmarks, and irregularities of pigmentation that may appear as pathological criteria or genetic idiosyncracies.

There are certain peculiarities about the color of organisms including man. Colors change with age. Hair becomes lighter until grey to white, or may fall out and reveal the color of the underlying skin. Skin becomes darker with exposure to the sun's rays. As with some other anatomical features there has been from ancient times an urge on the part of humans to tamper with their own coloration. Skin has been covered with white or red pigments; hair has been darkened, reddened, or bleached and some hair removed altogether. In spite of many numerous and inventive attempts to modify the color of the skin and hair these structures have been resistent and have eventually regained their unmodified hues. Color plays a vital part in human affairs: sociological as in the association of color with racial identity, aesthetic as in landscape and portrait painting and commercial as in the paint and cosmetic industries. It would therefore seem in order to examine in some detail the natural basis of coloring in the human body. We shall begin by reviewing briefly the biochemical and anatomical basis of color in the skin, hair, and eyes.

Five pigments occur in various parts of the body in differing concentrations and associations. These are *melanin, melanoid, carotene, hemoglobin* and *oxyhemoglobin* (Williams and Warwick 1980: 1219). Some of these are aspects or phases of others. The one with greatest variation and most dominating effect when in deeper concentrations is melanin.

Melanin: Melanin is a brown pigment that occurs in the skin, hair, eyes, and some of the internal organs. It is a dense brown polymer of the amino acid *tyrosine.* Tyrosine is converted through the action of the oxidizing enzyme *tyrosinase* into the final melanoprotein *melanin.* It is polymeric, has a high molecular weight, is insoluble in most solvents and has a complicated irregular chemical structure that is not completely known (Duchon, Fitzpatrick and Seiji 1968: 6 ff.). One chemical formula has been given as $C_{77}H_{98}O_{33}N_{14}S$ (Henderson and Henderson 1963). Melanin is stored in *melanosomes* that become a part of *melanocytes,* the pigment bearing cells in various parts of the body.

Melanoid results from the disintegration of melanin particles. It is a diffuse form of melanin and produces a yellow hue typical of the soles of the feet (Edwards and Duntley 1939: 12–13). *Carotene* is a yellow to orange pigment found in the skin, especially noticeable in female subjects. It occurs in tomatoes, squash, carrots, egg yolk and milk fat. When taken into the body it is stored in the liver and can be converted into vitamin A.

Hemoglobin. Hemoglobin is the red pigment in the blood. It consists of a protein *globin* combined with *heme,* an iron bearing substance based on a molecule consisting of carbon, nitrogen, hydrogen and iron. As the red blood cells are exposed to oxygen during respiration, they take on a bright red color. After these cells have given up their burden of oxygen in the lungs they become purple, the typical shade of venous blood.

Oxyhemoglobin is hemoglobin combined with oxygen. This form of hemoglobin produces the bright red color typical of arterial blood.

The Location of Pigments in the Human Body

Pigments occur in both the visible parts of human anatomy and in the internal structures of the body not normally seen. Our concern in this discussion is with the colors that can be seen and form the basis of personal recognition and racial identification. Pigments occur in various concentrations and combinations in the skin, hair, and eyes, all of which can be readily seen and are more or less difficult to modify or camouflage.

SKIN

Skin is the largest organ of the body and plays a highly important part in body functions. It also serves as a protective sheath for the muscular system, nerves, and internal organs, and helps to supply vitamin D. The surface area of the skin of an average male is calculated to be about 15,000 square centimeters. Skin varies in thickness with the part of the body in which it occurs, the thickness being proportional to the amount of pressure or friction to which it is subjected. The greatest thickness is on the dorsal surface of the neck and trunk and on the palms of hands and the soles of the feet. The thickness of the epidermis varies from three tenths of a millimeter to three millimeters and the thinnest is on the eyelids and the penis. The skin is the main receptor of external stimuli that approach the body, and is plentifully supplied with nerves. The skin of an average-sized person weighs around six pounds and is twenty one square feet in area.

The skin is the interface between the human body and the external world. The nerve receptors located in the skin report the sensations of heat or cold and the mechanical stresses and contacts to which the body is exposed. As the body passes through its cycle of daily events the skin receives and reports the scrapes, burns, and erotic contingencies involved in daily experience. It also serves as a barrier to the invasion of microorganisms, and aids in controlling body heat. Within the skin structure are the pigment cells. These may serve several purposes. They act as a buffer between the body and excessive ultraviolet radiation in the environment. In some situations these pigment cells create areas of protective camouflage patterns that are useful in avoiding disastrous contacts with predators and enemies. Also the flag of skin and hair color signals racial affiliation, friendship, or hostility.

The skin consists of two layers, the *dermis* or *corium*, which is covered by the *epidermis* (See Fig. 1). Deep in the epidermis is the layer of loose, irregular connective tissue that forms the subcutaneous layer. The epidermis is divided into four layers, from the outside inward the *stratum corneum*, or horny layer consisting largely of dead cells, the *stratum lucidum*, a thin clear layer, the *stratum granulosum*, and the *stratum germinativum* or *Malpighian layer*. The innermost layer, the stratum germinativum, contains melanocytes, the cells that synthesize melanin.

Skin color is the result of varied combinations and concentrations of melanin, hemoglobin, and carotene, plus some yellowing effect of the horny epidermal layer. The result of such variations in the proportions and arrangement of pigments is that human skin color is seen in a wide range of shades from deep brown, recognized as "black," to a pale reddish yellow, spoken of as "white." The principal determiner is the brown of melanin. An academic attempt has been made to classify humans as to pigmentation as follows: *melanoderms* or black skinned, *xanthoderms* or yellow skinned, and *leucoderms*, or white skinned. Such a classification is strictly artificial since there are no "pure" skin colors and the various shades of skin are blends of pigment colors and the effect of the outer epidermal layer plus the action of environmental conditions including radiation. Any dividing lines between the assumed basic skin colors are hypothetical for the convenience of description and cannot be satisfactorily applied to a blended series of characteristics. The visible color of skin of one person as viewed by another is a combination of effects produced by a number of factors. Melanin pigment is the dominating element in darker skinned peoples, but carotene, hemoglobin, and

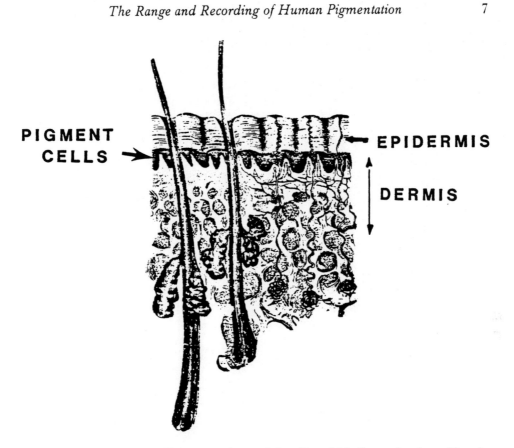

Figure 1. Section of Skin. The mucous layer of the skin, which lies under the epidermis, carries the melanin-bearing pigment cells. In addition to the melanin cells, the thickness of the epidermis and the blood in the dermal blood vessels affect the color of the skin.

oxyhemoglobin of the blood are important factors in some skin shades. The influence of blood color is regulated by the number and exposure of capillary blood vessels in a given area of skin. Skin color also may be influenced by the overlay of flattened cells in the outer layer of the skin, and this varies with the part of the body and is increased by friction in environmental contacts. These create a yellowish shade added to the other skin hues. The description of skin color for identification or other purposes has been a difficult and usually unsatisfactory undertaking. Skin color is hard to simulate through artists' pigments. Attempts to represent skin color in painting has often resulted in a crude and incondite effect unless applied by a highly skilled and proficient portrait painter. Efforts to describe skin color verbally have been unsatisfactory, because words for colors are vague and inspecific. What, for instance, is the meaning of "light brown"? To one person this might mean a shade called by another individual "tan," "yellowish brown," or "tawny." Anthropologists have struggled with this problem for over one hundred years.

Paul Broca (1824–1880), the French physician and anthropologist, who founded many of the techniques of physical anthropology, gave considerable attention to the shades of color in human skin, hair, and eyes. He devised a table that included samples of the colors recognized in the tissues of the body. His numbered samples ran from one to twenty for the eyes and from 21 to 54 for the skin. While his efforts and expertise developed a skillful procedure, outstanding for his time, Broca's methods involved obstacles in both field and laboratory investigations.

The American anthropologist who pioneered the science in the United States, Aleš Hrdlička, in his Manual of Anthropometry, first published in 1920 (Hrdlička 1920: 83), lists a classification of descriptive terms for skin color with four basic colors and 17 shades as follows:

DESCRIPTIVE TERMS FOR SKIN COLOR

Class of Color   *Shades*

WHITE—florid—light—medium—brunet—dusky—light brown. ·
YELLOW—pale yellowish or sallow—tawny (brownish yellow)—dusky
  yellow.
BROWN—light—medium—dark—chocolate (solid).
BLACK—brown black—bluish black—greyish black—ebony black.

Such visual comparison methods were never satisfactory. Differences in the visual acuity of observers, the quality of light under which the subjects were being viewed, and the physical state of the person being examined all introduced variables that made for unreliability and inconsistency in the findings. The need was felt for a method that would be independent of the observer's personal qualifications. The first step toward a more precise instrument for color designation was the color top (Sullivan 1928: 20–22). This was originally a toy, but with some modification it became a respectable device by which reflected colors could be measured, recorded and compared (See Fig. 2). It moved from the imperfect language of description to metrical observations (Davenport 1926: 44–49).

The color top consists of a spindle that can be rotated as a spinning top to which is attached a base disk. On this, four paper disks are mounted,

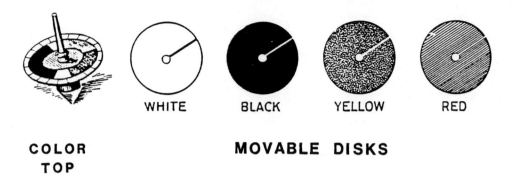

COLOR   MOVABLE DISKS
TOP

Figure 2. Color Top. The four disks of the color top can be turned in order to expose differing segments to the light. These are blended as the top whirls, creating a particular apparent color. The blend produced is defined by numerical calibrations around the circumference of the disk. While useful in creating a large series of apparent colors, the color top was not entirely satisfactory since the color produced was subject to variation with the quality of the light in the area and observations made varied with the visual acuity of the observer.

the disks being white, black, yellow, and red. Each disk has a slot so a portion of another disk can be exposed. By adjusting the disks, parts of several disks can be exposed at the same time. When the top is rotated rapidly, a blending of the exposed colors appears to take place as the observer looks at the whirling top. The base disk has around its outer edge a calibration so that the percentage proportions of each of the several colors can be noted in a formula consisting of abbreviations for the colors and a number representing the percentage exposed (Davenport 1926: 44–46). This method was a considerable improvement in the recording of colors, but it had serious shortcomings. In visually matching an area of human skin with the whirling disk the procedures were inconvenient and the same problem of human eye unreliability was involved as with earlier visual matching techniques (Todd, Blackwood, and Beecher 1928: 192–293).

Many of the inaccuracies in the previous techniques of skin color recording have been overcome by use of the *spectrophotometer* (Barnicot 1957: 114–116). This is an instrument that casts a beam of light on a skin area of the person being examined. The reflected light from this lighted area enters a sensitive photoelectric cell. This cell activates a recording device that indicates the percentage of reflectance, as compared with sunlight, of each wavelength of light that the cell receives (See Fig. 3). A graph resulting from the observations shows the percentage of reflectance to wavelength (See Fig. 4).

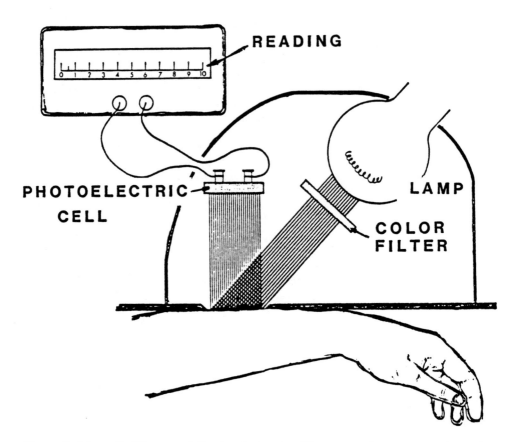

Figure 3. Schematic Diagram of Spectrophotometer. The spectrophotometer analyzes the color of reflected light in comparison with the colors of the spectrum. A photoelectric cell responds to the light reflected by the skin or hair of a subject being analyzed in a manner that can be read and recorded. (After Clarke)

There is no blue pigment in the skin and its related structures, but the effect of a blue appearance may in part result from the optical effect known as *scattering*. This results when a beam of light enters another substance and within this medium particles collide with and deflect some of the particles of the light beam. This may tend to raise the blue end of the reflected spectrum and diminish redness of the substance being viewed. This accounts for certain blue effects in the appearance of some skin areas. A noteworthy example of this is the *Mongolian spot, blue spot*, or *sacral spot* seen on the lower part of the back of many infants and young children. It occurs especially among many Mongoloid peoples including Chinese, Japanese, Koreans, Eskimos, and American Indians, but also occasionally may be seen in Negroes and the "white" races (Boyd

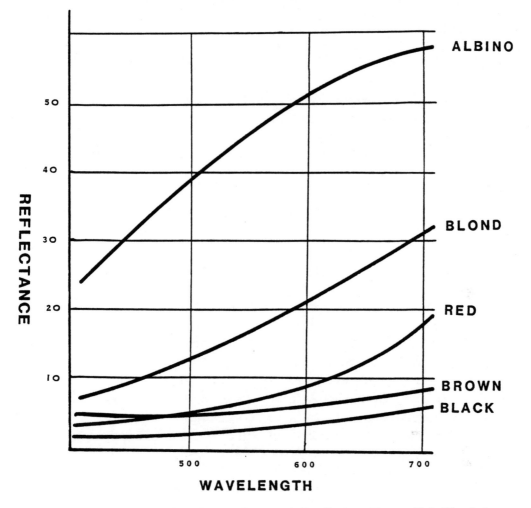

Figure 4. Graph Prepared from Spectrophotometric Readings on Human Hair. The darker hair absorbs more light than lighter hair and unpigmented albino hair has the highest reflectance.

1950: 313). The effect in other areas of the skin is sometimes noted, such as a man's face after having been closely shaven. Blue coloration in such circumstances is not the result of hemoglobin but the scattering of light beams as they enter a different medium, in this case the outer layer of the skin.

Variations in human pigmentation as observed or electronically recorded may occur for any of a number of reasons. The main reasons are:

Hereditary differences resulting from familial and racial genetics.

The history of the individual in terms of exposure to solar and other forms of radiation; also contact with chemicals that bleach or dye the skin.

The sex of the individual: females tend to be lighter than males.

The age of the person: children tend to be lighter than adults, and in advanced age the skin color changes, sometimes becoming lighter, in other cases darker than in earlier life.

The region of the body under observation: The less exposed parts of the body are lighter. The underside of the arm is usually chosen as the best area to observe skin color since it is largely protected from suntanning.

State of health of the person being observed: All over skin color and splotching are typical of certain diseases.

Environment at the time of observation: Time of day, amount and quality of sunlight, and objects that reflect light all may influence the coloration of the subject being observed. Skin pigmentation may be irregular rather than in the even grade of distribution commonly seen in darker skinned persons. In lighter skinned individuals the commonest type of irregular pigmentation is *freckling*. Freckles are not a pathological condition but are darker pigment spots that occur for no other reason than exposure to the sun. *Macules* or *maculae* are discolored spots or patches on the skin that are neither depressed or elevated with reference to the skin surface. They may be in various shapes and colors. They are associated with numerous body and skin disorders and are distinguished from *papules* that are elevated and usually red and are associated with a number of diseases, including measles, smallpox, and syphilis, and may develop after the use of certain medications.

HAIR

Hair, an important appendage of the skin, shares some of the skin's variety in color, but not all. Among mammals, hair has a variety of functions, both in regard to its presence and also its absence. One function is to conserve body heat by creating an envelope of air next to the skin. Another function is protective. A hairy coat offers a protective cushioning against blows and scrapes. Eyebrows and eyelashes provide accessory protection for the eyes. Through its pigmentation hair may provide camouflage, and its abundance, or at times its absence, may provide a sexually attractive role. In the human most of the proposed roles of hair have been limited or negative. There is scarcely enough hair on most humans to have much effect, either for heat conservation or protection. The eyebrows and eyelashes may play an occasional role in protecting the eyes, but probably not much under normal conditions. The camouflage role is probably limited to the lighter skinned peoples who may have had darker head hair or patches of lighter or darker body hair that made them somewhat less visible. This largely reduces the role of hair in humans to its part in sexual attractiveness. It is possible that ample hair on the face, or also the body, may in males have been a desirable characteristic and increased the chance of mating. It is perhaps equally possible that absence of hair on females, revealing the delicate color of the breasts and the face, may have been attractive to males and promoted the chance of mating. At least the bearded lady of the circus, although a striking curiosity, has not been remarkable for her enticing sexuality. It has been suggested that the reduced body and facial hair of females may have been an important factor in bringing about the reduction in hair or near naked state of many human races. The relative abundance of female head hair seems to have been the reverse of this. Abundant female hair has long been a symbol of erotic enticement. There well may have been a folkloristic connection between abundant head hair and fertility. Along with its color, long flowing hair may have been a potent fertility symbol (Cirlot 1952: 129–130).

There have been numerous suggestions as to the reason for the human's so-called "nakedness." One proposed theory is that man, like the aquatic mammals, has a layer of subcutaneous fat that insulates his body from the cold of his environment. In many mammals hair serves the purpose of insulation but in humans the fat layer serves this purpose and accordingly during the course of evolution body hair, being unneeded, tended to disappear (Mitchell and Patterson 1954: 83). It is difficult to reconcile this explanation with the highly abundant hairiness of the anthropoid apes. Another explanation that has been offered is that sexual selection was the cause: females that were less hairy were more desired by males and accordingly the less hairy hereditary types prevailed in the population. (The reader may wish to evaluate this in terms of the frequency of "electrolysis studios" in modern beauty salon complexes.)

Hair is a thread-like outgrowth of the epidermis of the skin. Each hair consists of a shaft and a root that develop from a bulb-like follicle of epidermal cells. Above the skin each hair consists of three layers: the outer cuticle, the cortex, which forms the bulk of the hair, and the central core or medulla, which may be hollow (See Fig. 5). Under the skin surface the hair expands to form a bulb that contains a matrix of dividing cells. When new cells are formed, the older ones are pushed upward to form the root and the shaft. Each hair is controlled to some extent by a small erector muscle attached to the follicle. This can raise the hair as a result of fright or other psychological stimuli. In the main part of the hair shaft the cells are elongated and flattened and contain pigment granules in dark hair, but air in white hair. A silvery appearance of the hair of older persons is due to reflection from air bubbles. Hair has been used as a basis of racial classification by earlier authorities (Deniker 1900: 285 ff).

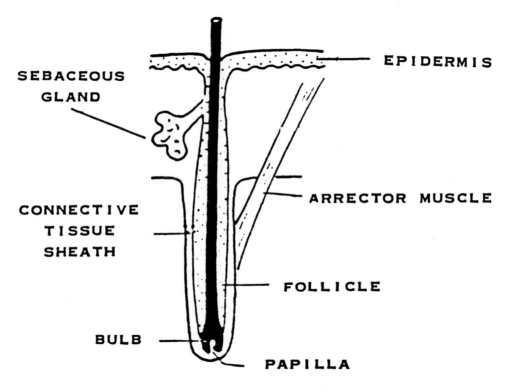

Figure 5. Diagrammatic Section of Hair and Scalp. The hair shaft emerges through the hair follicle and the connective tissue sheath to appear at the scalp surface. The shaft consists of three cell layers: the *cuticle*, the outer layer, the *cortex*, the main portion, and the *medulla*, the central axis. Elongated cells in the cortex contain pigment granules. White hair contains air bubbles rather than pigment.

Hair color has a wider range of variation than skin. Hair at the dark end of the range is extremely dark with the quality of "blue black." At the light end, hair is without pigmentation and appears white. The carotene pigment shows up to its maximum effect in hair. There are no red-haired races where the red pigmentation is universal, but red hair may be a familial hereditary trait in a number of light skinned populations.

There is a high correlation between the color of hair and eyebrows, but the correlation between the color of head hair and lashes is very low, almost nonexistent (Rozprým 1934: 395).

For anthropometric purposes a number of descriptive terms have been used for hair color. The classic American anthropometric manual (Hrdlička 1920) gives the following terminology:

Hair-Colors

Classes:

Blonds—Pigmentless, flaxen, straw, dull yellow, golden yellow; specials.
Intermediaries—Light brown, ashy, medium brown, medium reddish brown.
Brunets—Dark brown, near black.
Blacks—Rusty-black, bluish-black, coke-black, black.
Reds—Light brownish-red (sandy red), medium brownish-red, brick-red, saffron red, chestnut red (or auburn); specials.

One of the peculiar features of hair pigmentation is that hair pigments fade with the age of the individual and the hair usually becomes grey to white during middle age and beyond. Greying is noticeable among Europeans, usually from the mid-thirties, and among Negroes ten years later. How this occurs has been speculated about by a number of experts, and several theories have been proposed to explain this striking change. Four main theories have been stated. One is that pigmented hairs fall out and are replaced by unpigmented hairs. Another is that the medulla of each hair ingests the pigment cells and that these are carried off through the hair root. A third suggestion is that gas bubbles form that conceal the pigment cells. A fourth belief is that chemical reaction occurs in the hair that bleaches the pigment in the same way that bleaching takes place through the external application of hydrogen peroxide. The general acceptance of any one theory is yet to come about.

In physiological, and in particular forensic investigations, the question may arise as to the time involved for hair to change color: for strongly pigmented hair to turn grey or white. The rapid greying of hair has been dismissed by many authors as being impossible or "apocryphal"

(Mitchell and Patterson 1954: 84). It must be accepted that such greying of hair is rare, but there are reliable reports that under certain conditions it may occur (*J Amer Med Assn* vol 121, no 2, 1943, pp. 161–162). Cases are given where, as a result of physical or psychological stress, rapid greying can take place, perhaps overnight.

EYES

The eye is a highly complex organ, sensitive to the wavelengths of light that enter it from the person's environment (See Fig. 6). It contains, and holds momentarily for analysis, the images projected through its lens from the forms and color of the outer world. It leads impressions from the outer world through an elaborate nerve cable into the brain. The result is a minute image in the brain that registers form, color, and the subtle nuances of light and shade, texture, and perspective. The eye adjusts the direction of light beams that enter from the outside world as these fall upon its inner sensitive spherical surface, the *retina*. The retina is a complex expansion of numerous nerve endings to form a hemisphere with acute sensibility. The basic and elementary role of the retina is to record the absence or presence and intensity of light. During the course of organic evolution a further and more subtle function developed, the ability to distinguish light beams in their spatial interrelationship. This became the potential of vision that resulted in the ability to recognize an approaching figure on the landscape and the ability to read a printed page. To make this possible, a series of accessory structures came into play. A lens was needed to bring light beams into sharp focus in defining the form of the object seen. Moreover it was required that this lens be adjustable in its focal length in order to provide for various distances of the object reviewed. In addition, a provision was needed to adjust the amount of light received before it reached the retina. Excessive light was blinding; inadequate light was obscure. The answer to this requirement was the *iris*, a diaphragm with an exit hole which was automatically constricted or enlarged from one to eight millimeters in diameter as needed to control the light entering the eye. This interlock involved the retinal nerves and the muscles that control the iris, the eyelids, and the muscles surrounding the eye opening as well as those that activate the movements of the head.

The eyeball consists of three layers, the sclera, the choroid, and the retina (See Fig. 7). The sclera is a whitish, dense, fibrous structure, a

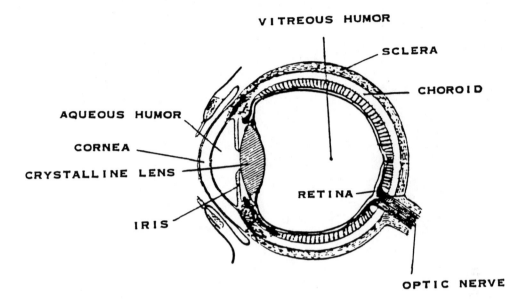

Figure 6. Section of Eyeball. Light entering the eye passes through the cornea, the aqueous humor, the opening in the iris, the crystalline lens, the vitreous humor and finally reaches the retina from which the stimulus passes through the optic nerve to the brain. In order to make vision possible, several adjustments must be made. The strength of the stimulus must be controlled. This is accomplished through the expansion and contraction of the iris, enlarging or reducing the opening through which the light passes. The iris contains the pigment cells that give the eye its color.

portion of which is seen as the "white of the eye." In the anterior portion of the eyeball this merges into a clear transparent lenticular disk, the *cornea.* The choroid is the middle layer of the eye structure, has many blood vessels, and is mainly nutritive in function. The retina is the inner layer that contains the rod and cone cells that are sensitive to light.

The "color of the eyes" results from the melanin cells in the iris. The external surface of the sclera is white, but the inner surface is brown. The sclera tends to have a blue tinge in childhood and to become yellowish in old age. A hereditary anomaly occasionally occurs in which the sclera is pale blue to grey blue in color. This is often found associated with fragility of the bones and with defective dentition.

The term *iris,* taken from the name of the Greek goddess of rainbows, is not entirely apt, since the range of color in the human iris is quite limited in comparison with the range of spectral colors. The shades of color in the human iris run from transparency through blues to various

SECTIONS OF IRIS

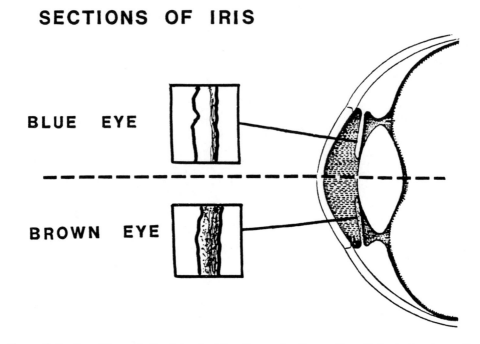

Figure 7. Sections Through the Iris of a Blue Eye and a Brown Eye. Melanin bearing cells create the brown coloration of a dark eye. In the blue eye the pigment cells are largely concentrated on the inner surface of the iris. Light passing through the translucent substance of the unpigmented portion produces the blue effect.

melanic hues to very dark brown, so-called black. The coloration is not always uniform, since flecks of various colors may occur, such as light brown, slate blue, grey, and green. Blue eyes have but little melanin in the iris. The blue effect is the result of some melanin cells located deeply in the structure of the iris. Light rays are reflected back through clear overlaying tissues.

Men's eyes are often darker than those of women (Olivier 1969: 77), but in some populations the opposite is true (Billy 1970: 355).

As with skin color, a descriptive terminology has been proposed for eye color. The classic American suggestion for this is Hrdlička's which is as follows (Hrdlička 1920):

EYE COLORS

Classes:

Blue—light ("forget-me-nots"), medium, rich blue, slate blue.

Subclasses

Green—often merely "greenish"; commonly associated with some brown; frequent in United States.

Gray—common among northern Slavs.

Brown—light, medium, dark, very dark.

Black—really extreme of brown, appearing black, in Negroes.

Conjunctiva—bluish, pearly white, yellowish, dirty or reddish yellow.

Iris color is inherited in Mendelian fashion with brown dominant and blue recessive. It is not sex linked and probably polygenic. It is associated with skin color, but not rigidly linked (Spooner 1957: 29).

A condition experienced in very early life or in old age is the occurrence of a greyish opaque ring on the iris, usually from 1.5 to 2 millimeters in width, near the periphery of the cornea. This, called the *arcus senilis* in the aged and *arcus juvenalis* in the young, results from a deposit of fat in the lamellae and corneal cells. It rarely invades the pupillary region. This ring considerably affects the overall appearance of the iris portion of the eye.

A review of the colors of human skin, hair, and eyes calls forth complex speculations. Some of these are dealt with later in this work. Perhaps the most important is how and when did coloration merge from an anatomical to a psychological issue? While color as a sociological consideration is beyond the scope of this work, one point of significance may be noted. Color, in its differing anatomic details, is an aspect of human variability. Variability leads to comparison and often competition and conflict. This may produce friendship or enmity, pride of ancestry, and a sense of superiority. The human's built-in anatomic variability, symbolized through color, has provided the groundwork for societal bonds of affiliation and stresses of conflict. At that point in human prehistoric development where differences in pigmentation became obvious, the sense of distinction between "our kind of people" and "suspect foreigners" entered into history.

Chapter 2

THE GEOGRAPHY OF PIGMENTATION

With advancements in the techniques of navigation and travel from the fifteenth century on, more and more parts of the world were explored and the inhabitants of these regions were described. The varieties of human physique were recorded and doctrines pertaining to the causes of these differences were propounded. Complex theories were advanced as to the differences in pigmentation. Doctrines were proposed as to the ability and quality of peoples as signalized by their skin, eye and hair color. Theories were set forth as to the cause of the coloring of human bodies in their differing environmental conditions. Some of the early speculations have continued into the dissertations of modern anthropology. Some have been proved fallacious and misleading. Our task here is to review briefly the range of human pigmentation in relation to location on the earth's surface, noting along with this the conditions of environment that occurred in various regions. The proposed evolutionary explanation of pigment differences will be reviewed in a later chapter.

Much of the earth's surface cannot support human life, except through complex cultural contrivance. The Arctic and Antarctic regions, high mountain and barren desert lands are inhabitable only through the use of specialized clothing and shelter, and carefully adapted food selection and preparation. In geographic terms this means that the theatre of human activity lies between 75 degrees north latitude and 60 degrees south latitude. Of this region a considerable portion is covered with salt water, some is arid and some so high that respiration is impaired. In other words human life has been practical in but a small segment of the planet and this segment consists of widely separated zones. The basic biological meaning of these facts is that as the human race emerged it became a number of isolated breeding segments kept more or less apart by the separation of areas capable of meeting the peculiar requirements of human physiology.

A superficial review of the human population in terms of pigmentary differences suggests that the worldwide range of melanic pigment in human skin extends from "black" to practically zero, without abrupt transitions. Carotene and hemoglobin also enter into the composition of human pigment systems, but the melanic brown component dominates except for the largely depigmented light end of the scale that includes blue eyes, yellow hair, and pink skin.

The Ancient Egyptians, in their painted sculptures and wall paintings, represented four human populations or "races," symbolized by pigment colors. The artists painted figures representing the Egyptians red, the Semites yellow, the Negroes black, and the Mediterranean peoples white (See Fig. 8).

EGYPTIAN   NEGRO
**   SEMITE   MEDITERRANEAN**

Figure 8. Ancient Egyptian Painting. The racial groups represented are symbolized by the colors red, yellow, black and white.

With the strong urge toward systematics in the nineteenth century anthropological studies a threefold classification of human races was adopted. Through combining data on body build, face form, nasal index, hair type, and other anatomical characters, patterns were developed for three primary races, the *Caucasoid, Mongoloid,* and *Negroid* (Haddon 1925: 7). Pigmentation was included but often did not harmonize well with the other criteria. Many of the earlier authorities gave skin color prime importance as a criterion of race classification and applied the terms *leucodermi,* or white skinned, *xanthodermi,* or yellow skinned and *melanodermi,* or brown skinned as basic racial types. It was eventually realized by most anthropologists that a dogmatic classification of races on the basis of a specific anatomic detail led to hopeless confusion since any one criterion of classification overlapped others in the distribution of populations. As peoples have spread through the habitable sections of the globe, interbreeding has blurred finite lines of classifying distinctions. Even so there are preponderant core areas where some basic characteristics appear largely to the exclusion of others. We can note that certain geographic areas are the homeland of particular pigmentation groups.

It is the purpose of the following discussion to note in concise terms the geography of human color, mainly as evidenced by the pigmentation of the skin, although other organs may manifest color shades, particularly the hair, and the iris of the eyes.

Before biochemical techniques for the study of human physiology were developed, involving blood types and their intricate classification, races were regarded as gross anatomical groups. It was eventually realized that the heredity of skin color is quite complex and that numerous genetic factors may be at work in determining the many shades of coloration. Also hybridization may result in varied hues of color and differing degrees of continued exposure to solar radiation may alter the observed color of the skin of individuals in certain areas of the body. Also it seemed quite clear that most aspects of human anatomical variability, including pigmentation, tend to pass through clines of gradation rather than show abrupt changes. Accordingly it seemed clear that the concept of "races" as discrete, well defined segments of the larger human population was untenable. Nevertheless the fact of human body variation is obvious, as is the fact that prior to the historically recent extensive migration of peoples, certain ranges of pigmentation were typical of geographical territories of the earth's surface.

A glance at the color distribution of mankind makes it clear that the darkest shades of brown occur between the 30th parallel north and 30th parallel south. This may be interpreted in several ways. A quick and overly simple explanation is that climate is the determiner of pigmentation; that the closer to the equator that people live the more exposure to solar radiation they receive and accordingly their skin has become darker through a progressive tanning effect, generation after generation. While attractively simple, this doctrine does not stand up under close analysis. In the first place it embodies the defects of the maxim of the inheritance of environmentally acquired characteristics. In the second place there are many exceptions to the principle in the facts of distribution: certain lighter skinned peoples have long resided on or near the equator. Some of the highland Papuans of New Guinea, who dwell near the equator, have pink skins and red hair (Coon 1969: 176). Also the New Caledonians in some cases have medium brown skin and blond hair. Some aboriginal Australians have blond hair, particularly children (Coon, Garn and Birdsell 1950: 80).

An often cited theory is that some mutations have tended to produce darker skin shades that offer protection against excessive radiation and, being favorable to survival, these traits became established. This proposed principle also faces some objections through the evidence of distribution. Unless a tenuous polygenetic doctrine of human origins is accepted it would be reasonable to assume that the ancestral population was of one color, probably light or medium brown, and that with the drifting apart of peoples to different environments some branches became lighter, others darker.

In applying either of the above hypotheses it would be necessary to postulate rapid genetic changes through environmental influence which is subject to objection on palaeontological grounds. In summary the geographical distribution of peoples does not clearly support any one theory as to the cause of skin color variation. Three basic facts do stand out, however, in considering the cartography of pigmentation.

1) The darkest pigmentation is found in the eastern hemisphere, south of the Tropic of Cancer and in Australia.
2) The medium skin toned people occur in North and South America, in Europe, and Asia north of the Tropic of Cancer. These vary from "white" to yellowish to light brown. Density of the skin is the main cause of the yellowish tinge characteristic of northeastern Asia. The lower the skin density the lighter the shade except that when the skin is less dense the blood in the capillaries creates a reddish color (Fleure 1927: 26–27).
3) People of the lightest coloration come from northern Europe.

The lightest of these peoples have but little melanic pigment in their skin, hair, and eyes, and approach the albinos in their lack of pigmentation but have some pigment in their pink skin, yellow hair and blue eyes. Some family lines among these peoples, however, have darker coloring, as among the Norwegians, Swedes, and some lineages of the British Isles.

Albinism, Albinoism or Albinismus

Quite rarely this pigmentation system is very weak or may approach zero. This results in a condition where the hair is white, the skin is delicately pink, and the iris of the eyes is pink or blue. The persons who experience these conditions are beset with a number of distressing problems. They have extremely sensitive skin and for comfort must wear clothing to protect their bodies from as much solar radiation as possible. Their eyes are particularly subject to irritation and damage from excessive ultraviolet radiation: they accordingly spend their outdoor lives wearing heavily tinted dark glasses. This condition is rare, occurring but once in 10,000 persons (McKusick 1964: 89). The cause is obscure, but the mechanism is understood. It results from a deficiency in the gene that controls the production and distribution of melanin throughout the normally pigmented parts of the body: the skin, hair, and eyes. It has been determined that this gene is transmitted through simple Mendelian inheritance and is usually recessive. Rarely, however, in some family lines, it appears to be dominant. It can occur in any race, but is more noticeable among darker skinned peoples.

A number of authorities have prepared maps designed to show the geographic distribution of skin color in the various populations of the world (Martin and Saller 1961: 1802; Brace and Montagu 1965: 272; Coon 1969: 210–211 after Biasutti). These various maps do not agree in many details since numerous difficulties beset the compiling of such a map. In the first place the data available for these compilations have been gathered by many individuals at different times, and population borders could have shifted considerably from time to time. Another obstacle has been in the verbal description of colors used in the ethnographic reports and travelers' accounts. Terms such as "medium light" and "medium brown" are subject to a wide range of interpretation.

In order to avoid such ambiguities it would be necessary to take spectrophotometric readings on the skin of representative persons from all the major areas represented in the maps, which would be a monumental task. The major portion of the inhabited earth is populated by peoples of the various intermediate grades of pigmentation. Whether this range of variability can be related significantly to solar radiation or other environmental factors is a matter of indeterminate speculation (See Map, Fig. 9).

Basically, pigmentation is the product of hereditary controls plus

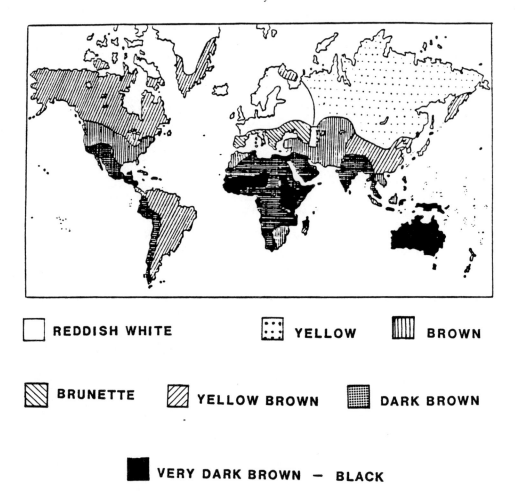

REDDISH WHITE   YELLOW   BROWN

BRUNETTE   YELLOW BROWN   DARK BROWN

VERY DARK BROWN — BLACK

Figure 9. Map Showing the Geographical Distribution of Skin Color (From Martin and Saller, after Walter). This is one of a number of efforts by respected authorities to prepare such a distribution map. None can be precise for the reason that the migration of peoples, racial crossing, and differing techniques of observation and recording have made firm geographic boundaries impossible to establish.

certain environmental influences that in each individual may override the hereditary determination. Occasionally the erratic behavior of genes results in vagaries or peculiarities that appear to be inconsistent with the normal expectation. Some of these interfere with the normal function of the organism and result in the early death of the individual. Others are neutral and have little if any survival value, but may result in atypical features that are noticeable as compared with the "normal" types. Among these latter are numerous pigmentary conditions, some of which are discussed in the next chapter. Some are merely sporadic deviations from normal expectancy for the population, such as the occurrence of lighter skinned peoples in a darker group.

Earlier investigators of human pigmentation felt that the cause of skin color variation could be surmised through a comparison between the maps showing the regional distribution of skin color with charts showing the range of temperature, solar radiation, and precipitation. From such a comparison it was believed that the influence of climate as a selective factor in determining the character and distribution of skin pigments could be established. For various reasons the findings from such comparisons proved unreliable. Skin color is a hereditary biological factor carried in the genetics of a population while climatic factors are physical phenomena subject to change in the natural environment. Except in a general way any noted similarity between the distribution of the shades of skin and the distribution of certain features of the climate is inconsistent and does not necessarily indicate a causal relationship. There is, certainly, a wide range in human pigmentation, but this variability results from complex body chemistry and cannot be explained simply through such forces as temperature and radiation. The skin of one generation could be tanned through exposure to the sun, but each descendant generation would require the same exposure for similar tanning.

Chapter 3

ATYPICAL PIGMENTATION

The basic physiological pigmentation of each human being is controlled by a number of hereditary genes. These determine the degree, type and area of pigmentation in the skin, hair and eyes. In normal hereditary transmission this pigmentation is usually symmetrical and conforms largely to the ancestral type of the individual. Occasionally, however, the hereditary mechanism becomes disarranged or is overridden by other internal or external forces, and peculiarities occur.

Atypical pigmentation can result from any one of four possible causes: (1) The hereditary determiners can become disarranged to the extent that colors in their shade, location or degree are contrary to the typical appearance of the persons affected, (2) Colors of the body can be influenced by internal physiological conditions such as pregnancy and aging, (3) Pigment changes may result from chemical or physical stimuli created by the environment, including extreme exposure to ultraviolet radiation, drugs used as medications, industrial or household chemical products, diet, or purposedly induced states such as tattooing and staining, (4) Certain diseases that affect other parts of the body can involve symptoms that include deviant colors of the skin. Examples of these several resulting conditions will now be given.

Freckling

Ephelis (pl. *ephelides*); *Lentigo* (pl. *lentigines*)
Melanic spots or macules of varying shades of red or brown. They may occur in any part of the body but are predominantly on the face, shoulder, and the anterior part of the chest. They are most numerous on persons with red or blond hair. They appear most markedly after exposure to x-ray radiation or frequent summer sun. They are uncommon in children prior to six years of age. There is a correlation between freckles and red hair, but none between freckles and the color of the iris of the eye (Cockayne 1933: 67).

29

Nevus Flammeus

One type of skin discoloration, a type that frequently affects the face, is a poorly defined dark red to blue area, often referred to as a "port wine stain." This is a *nevus* or *angioma* resulting from the hypertrophy of many small blood vessels. The smallest of such nevi is a "strawberry mark" that is bright red and slightly raised. This disappears early in life. The large port wine stain is an irregular area most often limited to one side of the face, usually smooth and hairless. It lasts throughout life but of itself has no harmful effect other than cosmetic. It may, however, be associated with pathological states. One is the Sturge-Weber syndrome, a form of angioma or clot of distended blood vessels overlaying and compressing the brain and may cause epilepsy. It usually occurs in a single member of a family but there are occasional exceptions (Cockayne 1933: 299).

Mongolian Spot

This is a variant of the blue nevus which occurs typically in the lumbosacral region although it may be in other areas including the chest, abdomen, face, and thighs. The spots are usually round or oval from 0.5 to 5 cm. in diameter. They are found in 1 to 5 percent of Caucasians although more frequently among Mongoloid peoples. They have been noted in 89 percent of Oriental infants up to one year of age (Allen 1967: 947). They have rarely if ever been found in persons with red or fair hair (Cockayne 1933: 69).

Age Changes

Changes in body coloration normally occur with aging. The process of whitening of the hair (*canities* or *leucotrichia*) is the most evident indication of aging through coloration. A yellowing of the skin accompanied by a harsh dry state (keratosis) is often typical of advancing years.

Blue Discoloration

Cyanosis is a bluish discoloration of the skin resulting from deficient oxygenation of the blood in the small blood vessels. It is most prominent in the hands and feet and also may be noted in the lips, cheeks, and ears. It may be congenital due to heart disease, but frequently results from certain drugs, especially sulphonamides, chlorates, and coal tar derivatives. It is associated with heart disease and pneumonia. A heliotrope or lilac blue color indicates a grave condition of the patient. "Blue babies" have the condition caused by partial asphyxia resulting from congenital defects in the heart.

Red Discoloration

Erythema is a redness diffused over a considerable area resulting from dilation of superficial capillaries. It may result from any one of a number of conditions. Both heat and cold may be the cause as well as penicillin, streptomycin, arsenicals, and coal tar derivatives. A variety of conditions loosely classed as "eczema" involves reddening of the skin directly caused by allergic reaction to poison ivy, poison oak and sumac, often exacerbated by scratching. There also may be psychosomatic causes.

Yellow Discoloration

Chlorosis is a yellowish or greenish grey discoloration of the skin usually occurring in young females as a result of iron deficiency, poor hygiene, and deficient diet. It is becoming rare.

Contact Dermatitis

This is a common condition resulting from industrial irritations and exposure to chemicals. It has many manifestations and possible causes. One percent of all factory workers have occupational dermatitis and 20 percent suffer from hypersensitivity or allergy. Others are stressed by nonallergic irritative agents. An allergic subject may show allergic dermatitis from such allergins as wood dust, spices, flour and caster pumice, also rubber, plastics, clothing dyes, detergents, and insecticides (Allen 1967: 227). Another type of contact dermatitis is caused by acids, alkalis, and petroleum products such as soaps and detergents. All of these may provoke itching and redness.

Skin Color Affected by Metallic Substances

Exposure to and contact with metallic substances can affect body pigmentation. A few of the more common of these are as follows:

Gold salts can produce eruptions and dermatitis.
Bismuth may produce slate color and blue black gum lines.
Mercury can result in a dirty appearing, slate grey pigmentation, especially on the eyelids, face and neck.
Arsenic may cause the skin to darken.
Silver is resistant to acetic acid and has various industrial applications,

such as photography and dental amalgams. Exposure to silver salts may result in *argyria* that produces an ashen grey color of the skin and conjunctiva of the eyes (Hunter 1969: 412).

Yellowing of the Skin

Xanthosis is a yellowing of the skin resulting from excessive quantities of carrots, squash, egg yolk, and other foods containing carotenoids in the diet. The reaction is readily reversible. A similar reaction results from taking *atabrine*, a form of *quinacrine hydrochloride*, used in the treatment of malaria and tapeworm. Other drugs reported as causing increased pigmentation include methotrexate, cytoxan, dibromomannitol, and procarbazine (Fitzpatrick, Wick and Toda 1926: 200).

Melasma is an atypical light to dark brown coloration of the face, neck, and at times the forearm. It is aggravated by sunlight. Its cause is variously assigned: it sometimes seems to be hereditary although oral contraceptives, estrogen, progesterone, and a number of cosmetic preparations have been cited (Pathak, Madhu A., in Fitzpatrick, Wick and Toda 1986: 161–172).

A form of induced skin discoloration of possible forensic significance may be noted. A carotinoid drug, canthexanthin, when taken daily in doses of 120 mg., produces a salmon pinkish color of the face, closely resembling a suntanned effect. This has been used as a cosmetic, helping to provide a fashionable outdoor life style appearance, but also may provide a distracting characteristic in personal identification.

Intentional Color Modification

The purposeful coloring and decoration of the skin through the tattooing of designs and emblems with colored dyes has been a compelling fad from antiquity to the present. Several methods of tattooing have been developed (See Fig. 10). The most common has been the piercing of the skin with a series of punctures created by thorns, spines, or metal points driven into the skin either through manual pressure or by mechanical means. Pigments, consisting mainly of lamp black and powdered charcoal for black, indigo from plants, carmine from insects (cochineal), and red from mercuric sulfide (cinnabar), are either applied by the piercing points as these are inserted in the skin or rubbed in later. A second method involves the cutting of a groove or furrow with a chisel-shaped instrument after which pigments are applied. A third method requires making deep cuts in the skin in which scars are formed that appear light colored on the dark skin, needing no further pigment application. A fourth method involves making wounds by various means after which healing leaves raised scars. The first method, that of a series of punctures, is most commonly encountered. The latter three procedures are essentially those of various aboriginal peoples often being a part of rituals symbolizing tribal affiliation, the attainment of manhood or other social rites.

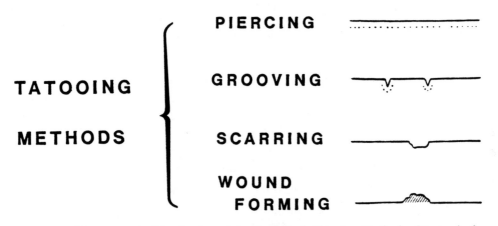

Figure 10. Diagrammatic Skin Section of the Four Basic Tatooing Methods. *Piercing* is the most common, being usually made with a needle or a thorn. This, and *grooving,* usually involve the application of pigments to the incised flesh. *Scarring* and *wound forming* do not necessarily involve the addition of pigments since scar tissue creates the desired pattern. Modern decorative tatooing is a form of mechanized piercing.

The effect of tattooing is not limited to colored lines and areas in the design but may involve reactions from the dyes and the physical injury involved in the injections. Inflammation may develop in the operated area.

Induced Pigment Modifications

There are two primary reasons for tampering with the natural coloration of the human face and hair. First, in frequency, is the compelling urge to comply with the trend of fashion, whatever this may be. In the female segment of the population this usually includes heightening the color of the cheeks and lips and stressing the outline of the eyes. These forms of artifice go well back into antiquity as is witnessed by Egyptian sculptures (See Fig. 11). Another motive for altering the color of the body is the desire or assumed necessity for obscuring the personal identity of the individual. Efforts toward the latter end may include staining the skin of the face, hands, and arms, altering the color of the hair, and concealing the color of the iris of the eyes by means of contact lenses with opaque shades of brown, blue, lavender, or green.

The human body offers several convenient possibilities for alteration of the original pigmentation. Hair, in particular, is subject to relatively easy modification through either bleaching or dying. A blond person can become a brunette through dying the hair and wearing dark colored contact lenses, while a dark brunette may become a blond through a simple cosmetic procedure involving hydrogen peroxide or chlorine and wearing blue shaded contact lenses. These very effective techniques are of practical interest to the cosmetic industry, to the cosmetological profession, and to forensic investigators who deal with the problems of personal identification. Nature cooperates in such endeavors by providing surfaces on the face for convenient application of prepared pigments, and hair that responds readily to chemicals that bleach or darken.

To be born with a certain hereditary endowment as to pigmentation does not necessarily mean that a person may live throughout his life without numerous modifications of this. Age, disease, occupational and other stresses and the impact of daily experiences, including purposeful alteration, may modify the shades of color that we see in the skin, hair, and eyes of our associates. Color is an important ingredient in the processes of human interrelationship, but is not necessarily a lifetime feature of human anatomy.

Discoloration Resulting from Body Disorders

Abnormal discoloration of the skin is associated with a large number of body disorders. The color may range through a variety of shades of yellow, brown, red, and green. The term *jaundice* or *icterus* is applied to a yellow condition of the skin and the eyes. It is not a disease in itself but is a symptom of any one of a number of disorders of the liver, gallbladder, and the blood. One cause is the blockage of the bile duct by a gallstone, resulting in the accumulation of bile in the bloodstream.

Malingerers have sometimes taken doses of picric acid (trinitrophenol) commonly used as a dye or an antiseptic. Ingestion of this causes the skin to take on a yellowish color resembling that typical of one of the jaundice disorders and hence may be used as a plea for exemption from military or other duties.

Addison's Disease

Alteration of the normal skin color is typical of *Addison's disease.* This is a disorder due to the inadequate secretion of the corticosteroid hor-

Figure 11. Ancient Egyptian Eye Makeup. Egyptian paintings, particularly those of the eighteenth dynasty, show facial details of their subjects in formal and definite style. One consistent characteristic is the outlining and extension of the feminine eye opening through painting with a dark line. This heritage of ancient Egypt seems often to survive in the twentieth century A.D.

mones of the adrenal glands. The skin color ranges through all shades of brown. The pigmentation may be blotchy or evenly distributed. In a case of Addison's disease a Caucasian is said to be often taken for a mulatto. The disease is rare, only about four persons in a million being affected.

Darier's Disease

Darier's disease or *keratosis follicularis* is a condition of unknown cause in which patches of crusted papules form, particularly on the trunk, face and scalp. These eventually become grey or grey brown to purple.

Vitiligo

Vitiligo or *leukoderma* is a deficiently pigmented condition of the skin and sometimes the hair as well. The hands, face, and neck are the most commonly affected areas. The depigmented patches are large or small, are static or progressive, and are sharply defined. The cause of this condition is unknown. It may follow pinta, syphilis, or psoriasis, and may result from irritants such as rubber dust in which an antioxidant has been mixed. The wearing of heavy rubber gloves has been cited as a cause (Allen 1967: 685).

Gastrointestinal Tumors

Malignant tumors of the gastrointestinal tract may produce flushing of the face with a reddish hue. The flushing episode may be temporary, lasting from one to thirty minutes, or may be a constant condition.

Pinta

One of the most dramatic of the pathological conditions that affect the pigmentation of the body is the treponemic disease *pinta,* also called *carate* in Colombia, *mal de pinto* in Mexico, *azul* in Chile and *boussarole* in Haiti. It is endemic to tropical America and is caused by a spirochete *Treponema carateum.* A large papule develops on the face, hands or other exposed areas. The smaller papules coalesce and take on various colors from red to deep blue (Allen 1967: 469–473). In the secondary stage the colors vary from white, grey and yellow to red, purple, brown, and black pigmented areas. There may be large irregular areas that remain depigmented. It has been reported in Haiti, the Dominican Republic, Puerto Rico, Venezuela, Ecuador, Mexico, and Cuba.

As has been just reviewed, the coloration of the human body can be caused by many other factors than heredity, and may have other than "racial" origins. From the practical forensic viewpoint it is important to bear in mind that colors seen on the face, hair, and eyes of a person may deceptively suggest a racial affiliation or a personal identity that does not exist. Such misleading hues of color may be the result of fortuitous environmental influences, a unique physiological occurrence, or an intentional manipulation for conformity to style or to avoid personal recognition.

Chapter 4

PIGMENTS, ADAPTATION
AND HUMAN EVOLUTION

When reviewing the range of pigmentation in mankind, from dark
brown ("black") through varying shades of brown and mixtures
with red, to "white," to depigmented albinism, it is difficult to avoid
speculations as to how it came about that in one species so many forms of
coloration developed.

Charles Darwin's evolutionary hypothesis held that through natural
selection the various forms of environment furthered the survival of
certain characteristics that in some way helped their possessors deal with
the problems and events that they faced in their daily existence. Prior to
Charles Darwin's researches, Buffon and Lamarck had attributed variations in animal structure to the impact of environment: the effect of
surroundings and conditions of living created changes in body tissue
that were passed by heredity through succeeding generations. Buffon felt
that this was by means of a direct effect on the external structure of the
body; Lamarck believed that in animals the effect was internal, through
the effect of environmental impact carried out within the nervous system.
According to either doctrine, the darkening of the skin was assumed to
result from the cumulative effect of suntanning by exposure or other
environmental conditions through successive generations.

It was gradually realized that the "inheritance of acquired characteristics"
involved too rapid changes and was an untenable doctrine. It did not fit
the facts of the gradually unfolding history of life and it was unacceptable
in view of the increasing appreciation of the age of the earth through the
growing sciences of geology and palaeontology. A more plausible explanation emerged through the natural selection principle of Charles Darwin.
The belief he presented was that, during the course of nature, organisms
may not precisely replicate, generation after generation, but that deviations or *mutations* from time to time may occur. Many of these variations
may have been of no value to their possessors, but a few have given those

individuals in which they occur an advantage over others. Those who
have the favorable genes in their heredity survive in greater vitality and
in greater numbers than the others in the same generation.

If this doctrine is applied to skin color, the variants toward darker skin
would presumably be favored for survival if the darker skin acted as a
shield against excessive and harmful ultraviolet radiation, and provided
better adaptation in areas where clear skies made for consistent exposure
to sunlight. The reverse may have applied in a northern climate where
sunlight was obscured by hazy skies resulting in an unfavorable reduction in the amount of solar radiation. This simple explanation seemed
adequate for many of the more elementary interpreters of Darwin who
felt that variations in skin color, hair and eye color could be adequately
explained by it. In a careful study of the principle in its presumed
applications certain problems began to appear. By the strict application
of this doctrine there should be a steady increase in depth of pigmentation from northern latitudes toward the equator. This did not always
seem to have been the case. Also the fundamental tenet that melanin in
the skin has adaptive value in blocking harmful solar radiation has been
brought into question (Riley 1977: 79).

With increased knowledge of the world's peoples and better techniques of observation, this distribution failed to conform consistently to
the model. In the New World the Eskimo of the far north are as dark as
many peoples of the equatorial area, and the Punan of Borneo who live
on the equator are much lighter than the Australian natives who live
much farther south. Any attempt to explain the pigmentation of the skin,
hair, or eyes solely on the basis of solar radiation or moisture is beset
with numerous exceptions. In support of the climatic determination
theory the explanation for exceptions usually offered is that there have
been recent migrations of peoples and that light skinned peoples now
living in tropical areas have not lived long enough in the regions
needing protection from ultraviolet radiation for the process of mutation
and selection to have taken effect. With advances in dating techniques
many areas of human development are older than had been previously
assumed and more time has been available for evolutionary change than
had been assumed with shorter chronologies. How much time was needed
to elaborate a primitive racial stock into a varied expression as seen
today in the many branches of *Homo sapiens* is difficult to estimate, but
successive mutations required to develop dark brown skin from pale skin
or from brown eyes to blue eyes must have been considerable. Mutation

is rare and it is estimated that only one germ cell in a hundred thousand or a million may carry a mutated form (Mather 1964: 37).

The cause and nature of random heritable variations or mutations has been a subject for extensive investigations and is being gradually clarified through investigations in molecular genetics. It has been established that the genes or units of heredity consist of the complex chemical DNA (deoxyriobonucleic acid). This in its essential constitution is normally transmitted precisely from generation to generation, but occasionally a discontinuity or "mistake" occurs that results in a different characteristic. These new combinations are held together by a protective mechanism that maintains the new gene structure through ongoing generations until another mutation may revise the genic structure.

In applying the principles of organic evolution to human pigmentation, certain queries arise in interpreting the basic hypotheses:

Skin color: What differentiates fitness from less fitness grades? In which climates? How much of a handicap is a presumably less fit condition?

Hair color: Is hair color a significant factor in shielding against ultraviolet radiation? Are skin color and hair color connected as a protective system?

Eye color: Is the pigmentation of the iris a significant protection of the deeper structures of the eye?

The camouflage factor: Do skin, hair, and eye color form a meaningful cluster of traits that make the individual less visible when this is an advantage?

Each of these questions will now be examined in greater detail.

A question with regard to the character of human skin and hair pigmentation is the probable color of the ancestral primate from which the various races of mankind descended. Was the human ancestor medium brown skinned and did some of his descendant stocks become lighter as the need for more ample solar radiation developed when they moved away from tropical environments, and did some of the descendant lines become darker to "black" in adaptation to climates of more intense solar radiation? Or perhaps was ancestral man very dark and did descendant strains take on various lighter shades of skin with migration into regions of the earth with less solar radiation? Such debates can become litigious and interminable with little result except to emphasize the complexity of biological phenomena. Not much if any help toward an answer can be obtained through reviewing the pigmentation of the anthropoids related to man. Man's closest primate relatives are the chimpanzee and the gorilla, which live in quite similar environments in Uganda. Yet the gorilla's skin is very dark brown and that of the chimpanzee is light. Numerous examples make it impossible to explain pigmentation differences on any simple basis. Washburn summarizes this: "Face color in monkeys and apes does not correlate in any simple way with environment, and I suspect that the same will prove to be the case with man (Washburn 1964: 1174).

Pigmentation is basically controlled by genetic inheritance. At times environmental conditions can create states that closely resemble those brought about through mutations and selection. Such *phenocopies* can be confused with genetically induced conditions and lead to mistaken evolutionary explanations. Also some dark skinned peoples may be somewhat protected from ultraviolet solar radiation by clothing and a cover of forest overgrowth in their living areas. Two populations of the same genetic inheritance for skin color may accordingly differ in the expressed hue of skin color. Through suntanning, a light skinned person by heredity may take on a darker color similar to that of individuals with hereditary brown skin. If deeper pigmentation in tropical environments were to be attributed entirely to selection involving the protective effect of melanin in the skin, in the past the darker skinned peoples would have consistently left more offspring than those of lighter skinned population groups, which has not always been the case. A propensity toward suntanning is largely an individual variable and it is not a racial characteristic (Lee and Lasker 1959: 252–259). Moreover, the conditions resulting from excessive radiation, such as skin cancer, develop mainly after middle age, past the age of primary reproductive activity (Lewonton 1982: 126). Another factor in the environment that possibly has had a considerable effect on the selection mechanisms that determine the grade of skin color is the development of agriculture. This provides a perennial food supply, with only seasonal requirements for intensive exposure to solar radiation. By contrast the hunter was compelled to expose himself to the elements throughout the year at prolonged intervals in order to survive. The village dweller practicing even an early form of agriculture could survive for considerable periods on stored food and devote himself to sedentary tasks under the protective shade of trees and his habitation (Buettner-Janusch 1973: 483–484).

Variation in skin color has been attributed to other environmental elements than ultraviolet radiation, mainly heat loss and moisture.

In human physiology it is vitally important that the basic internal temperature of the body, the *core temperature*, be kept at a close range of around 98.6 degrees F. Oral temperatures range from 96.6 to 100.0 degrees F (35.8 to 37.8 C) among healthy persons (Best and Taylor 1966: 1413). This is accomplished in a variety of environments through a number of mechanisms. The rate of heat loss must be adjusted to the metabolic production of heat. If the surrounding temperature falls, the metabolic production of heat must be increased. Shivering is a part of the method by which this is accomplished. On the other hand, if the external temperature rises, methods must go into action that bring down the body temperature. These include the evaporation of sweat. In general heat is produced metabolically by the muscles and viscera of the body and is transferred by the flow of blood. A body absorbs heat from an environment with higher temperature than its own. It has been maintained that by screening the body from external heat sources darker skin decreases the thermal adjustment load on the body, making thermal adjustment easier in warm to hot surroundings. On the other side of this contention, it should be noted that dark skin absorbs heat and light skin reflects it, producing less effect on the internal systems. This brings up a significant paradox. In a warm environment the dark skin absorbs heat, much of which may not be needed; in a cool environment the light skin reflects . heat that is needed.

One proposed explanation of the development of dark skin is that dark brown skin color provides camouflage during hunting and warfare. The argument is that a dark skinned person in a shaded environment is less visible than a lighter skinned individual to enemy warriors and attacking carnivorous animals. It is true that dark skin absorbs more light than light skin and this reduces its visibility in a dark environment. It is also true that the coloration of animals other than man usually involves blotches or stripes rather than solid color areas (Cowles 1959: 286). To be effective, any camouflage must closely resemble the environment and offer few unbroken lines of demarcation. Humans during hunting or fighting are rarely in a solid dark brown environment. During jungle warfare the uniforms most protective are colored green and brown in irregular camouflage areas.

From the preceding review it can be seen that theories as to the evolution of skin color are a subject of entertaining speculation rather than scientific assurance. Many peoples, regardless of their skin color, have carried on a reasonably successful way of life in quite different environments. Blond peoples have migrated to the tropics and very dark skinned peoples from ancient times have settled in Tasmania, New Zealand, and India. The mid range yellow brown populations have been well adjusted to life from the equator to Siberia and Tierra del Fuego. What seems quite certain is that the human organism, through its numerous adjustive physiological mechanisms plus some adaptive cultural aids, has been able to survive and propagate in a variety of climates. To what extent these climates have acted as a selective agency in creating genic differences in population groups is far from certain and awaits further research for a satisfactory resolution. Much is yet to be learned as to the effect of solar radiation on the human body and the sources of radiation in the atmosphere and the materials of the earth's surface.

Hair and Eyes

The color of hair and that of the eyes are often thought to be involved in the same selective processes as the skin (Daniels 1964: 982). The anatomy and biochemistry of these structures is quite complicated, and in many instances their pigmentation seems contradictory. Hair seems to follow the tendency of skin color, but many exceptions occur. Dark skinned persons will normally have dark hair but a dark skinned person can have blue eyes and a light blond individual will occasionally have brown eyes. Such combinations may present exciting possibilities for mating and may create curiosities in the area of human genetics. Eye color is probably the most difficult area of pigmentation to explain on the basis of environmental adaptation. Without question the effect of long exposure to bright sunlight damages the tissues of the eye, causing burning of the eyes, eyestrain, and perhaps cataracts, and partial or total blindness. Yet it is probably unjustified to propose that this condition is particularly aggravated in the tropics and that this led to darker eyes as a hereditary protective feature. In the first place life in the tropics does not necessarily involve long periods of exposure to direct solar radiation. Heavy vegetation with numerous trees and thick overgrowth often creates a natural protection for dwellers in these areas during many of their activities. In the second place, peoples who have lived for a long time in tropical environments have learned to adjust their regimen of daily living to the sunshine cycle, and do not "go out in the noonday sun." In the northern latitudes during the cold season the ground is snow-covered much of the year during which light reflected by the snow reinforces the direct radiation in the atmosphere. The ultraviolet light rays in such exposure can burn the cornea and other structures of the eye causing painful snowblindness (Gifford 1942: 382). The Eskimo make "snow eyes," goggles fashioned of wood or bone that restrict the amount of light entering the eye but permit viewing through a narrow open slit. The Eskimo have dark brown eyes, but northern European peoples who have dealt with many of the same conditions have blue eyes. Repeated snow blindness among the Eskimo appears to result in a condition ranging from light brown to blue eyes (Jenness 1921: 259–260).

It is difficult to make a convincing case for environmental selection in the evolution of light eye color other than to assume that a lessened pigmentation involving both skin color and eye color may have provided some slight advantage in regions where the annual exposure to solar radiation has not been adequate to provide the vitamin D needed by the body.

Both hair and eye color may in some populations have been influenced by sexual selection. To what degree pigmentation may have been a factor in choosing a particular mate among several possibilities is a subtle matter that involves the psychological mechanisms of aesthetics, fashion, prestige, and whim, all of which are impossible to analyze satisfactorily among contemporary individuals, and are certainly beyond the scope of reliable interpretation for prehistoric peoples.

The most striking and vivid pigmentation seen in humans is red hair. It is difficult to imagine that this had any survival value in human evolution other than perhaps an occasional sexual selective role. It is not related to climate, and seems to be a recessive trait (Clegg 1958: 78). European peoples have the greatest diversity of hair color, but, among these, red hair is relatively rare. It is often seen among Scottish Highlanders, Welsh, Irish, and Finns, but is far from universal even in these racial groups.

It is statistically established that the dark pigmentation of Negroes is negatively associated with the incidence of skin cancer. It was assumed for a considerable time that the melanin in dark skin acts as a protective shield against excessive exposure to ultraviolet radiation, and that this reduced the hazards of exposure to the sun as a cause of cancer. Also, skin cancer incidence is higher among individuals whose occupation requires them to be exposed for long periods to sunlight and so have skins darkened more than among those not so exposed (Taussig and Williams 1940: 729–730). Yet, however, melanin is not in itself the reason for reduced cancer susceptibility among Negroes. Negroes do not show a comparable immunity to other types of cancer, so various aspects of the skin are probably involved. Skin cancers are usually not lethal and occur later in life than the normal time for mating. For these reasons it would seem unlikely that dark skin as a protective device against exposure that may cause cancer can be considered as a major selective force in the course of human evolution (Blum 1961: 56–57).

An important but confusing issue with regard to the evolution of human pigmentation is the relative role of diet and sunlight as causes of the disease of rickets in children, or the related osteomalacia in adults. This disease produces swollen ends of long bones, bow legs, knock knees, and pain in walking. It was found in some situations that children living in dark, unlit areas, such as in crowded industrial cities, and in regions with long winters, are more prone to rickets than those who live in areas more open and better exposed to sunlight. It was also found that fish oil, egg yolks and other vitamin D containing foods arrest this condition. It was furthermore found that even in areas of poor nutrition children who live largely in the open do not develop rickets. Two schools of thought have emerged among investigators, the "Glasgow school" and the "London school." The Glasgow group, through animal research, found that pups kept in the open were free of rickets, but those kept in a laboratory developed the condition. The London group held, from their investigations in India, that nutrition was the key to the condition (Loomis 1970: 80). With time it was learned that both viewpoints may be correct, since a lack of vitamin D, either through dietary deficiency or inadequate exposure to sunlight may be the cause. Also there are several types of rickets with somewhat different causal conditions.

The essence of the rickets issue with regard to the evolution of human pigmentation is merely this: Was there selective significance in conditions where rickets occurs and if so what were the evidences of these conditions? Also, were the antirickets conditions associated with skin color? The answers are unfortunately vague and are based on physiological issues that are as yet not thoroughly explored to the satisfaction of experts. This much may be stated as a guideline to speculations:

The masking of sunlight, either through the concentration of melanin or the thickening of tissues through which light must pass, can withhold the action of violet ray impact. Whether this is good or bad for survival depends on the climate in which the individual has lived or continues to live. Obviously rickets and its associated pathological conditions are undesirable and burdensome as a device for dealing with the problems of survival. These conditions have occurred in a variety of forms, some of which have been in the long run lethal to their possessors, and others have been of little survival significance.

In an attempt to assemble data and theories in regard to the evolutionary role of body pigments, it may be noted that there may be validity in the belief that skin color may have played some part as a shield against excessive ultraviolet actinic radiation from the sun and that darker skinned persons may have survived longer and reproduced more ably in certain areas for this reason. Yet quantitative evidences for this are problematical. Hair pigmentation would probably have had very little effect in this regard and the color of the iris of the eye still less.

It is perhaps fitting that this discussion close with a statement made a century ago by Charles Darwin, the founder of much that we now know as evolutionary biology.

> Of all the differences between the races of man, the colour of the skin is the most conspicuous and one of the best marked. It was formerly thought that differences of this kind could be accounted for by long exposure to different climates; but Pallas first shewed that this is not tenable, and he has since been followed by almost all anthropologists. This view has been rejected chiefly because the distribution of the variously coloured races, most of whom must have long inhabited their present homes, does not coincide with corresponding differences of climate. (Darwin, Charles 1896: 192)

The process of organic evolution has not been a rigorously logical regimen and although the neat reasoning of Charles Darwin may have obtained in many areas, some of its trends may have occurred through accidental and fortuitous innovations. It is quite possible that pigmentation may have developed trends in this category (Fitzpatrick, Wick and Toda 1986: 29). Adventitious trends may have been strengthened and directed by forces other than biological advantage. Aesthetic considerations, social and political expediency, and prevailing styles may not always have harmonized with the best details for biological survival. The development of culture could have introduced nonbiological elements in the evolutionary selective process. It is impossible to know at what point in human evolution culture may have played a part, if any, in the selective roles of pigmentation, but this possibility cannot be excluded.

Colors figure strongly in the language, factual and figurative, of human communication. The terms for shades of color often have obvious psychological associations. Some of these are reflections of the anatomical pigmentation of the body. If you say that "you feel blue today," the phrase may have been suggested by the color of stagnant blood, but if a person is said to be "red blooded" this may have been suggested by the red arterial blood spurting vigorously from a wound. The origin of such terms as "yellow" to mean cowardly, "green" to mean unskilled and inexperienced, "white" to mean fair and friendly, "purple with rage," "white with fear," "brown study," "dark look," "pink of condition," and "see red," are open to speculation, but we can reasonably assume that many of these terms were involved with human coloration, temporary or permanent. We can readily surmise that, from the remote prehistoric past, the human body in its varied conditions was a palette of many shades that were reacted to, modified, displayed or hidden, according to the psychology and physiology of the individual.

BIBLIOGRAPHY

Allen, Arthur C. 1967. *The skin: a clinico pathological treatise.* 2nd ed. New York and London: Grune & Stratton.

Babun, Edward. 1969. *The varieties of man.* London: Crowell-Collier.

Baker, Paul T., and Weiner, J. S., eds. 1966. *The biology of human adaptability.* Oxford: Clarendon.

Barnicot, N. A. 1957. Human pigmentation. *Man 57:* 114–120.

Beeson, Paul B., McDermott, Walsh, and Wyngaarden, James B. 1979. *Cecil textbook of medicine.* Philadelphia, London, Toronto: W. B. Saunders.

Best, Charles Herbert, and Taylor, Norman Burke. 1966. *The physiological basis of medical practice.* 8th ed. Baltimore: Williams & Wilkins.

Bettmann, S. 1932. Haut und Konstitution. *Zeit für Konstitutionslehre 16:* 485–501.

Billy, Ginette. 1970. Nouvelles Données sur l'Evolution contemporainne des Parame tres raciaux. III La Pigmentation de l'Iris. *L'Anthropol 74:* 353–374.

Borrie, Peter, ed. 1971. *Modern trends in dermatology — 4.* London: Butterworths.

Blackwood, B. 1930. Racial differences in skin-color as recorded by color top. *J Roy Anthropol Inst 60:* 137–168.

Bleibtreu, Hermann K., and Downs, James F. 1971. *Readings in physical anthropology.* Beverly Hills, California: Glencoe.

Blum, Harold F. 1961. Does the melanin pigment of human skin have adaptive value? an essay in human ecology and the evolution of race. *Q Rev Biol 36:* 50–63.

Boyd, William C. 1950. *Genetics and the races of man: an introduction to physical anthropology.* Boston: Little, Brown.

Brace, C. L., and Montagu, M. F. Ashley. 1965. *Man's evolution.* New York: Macmillan.

Broca, Paul. 1865. Instructiones générales sur anthropologiques: usage du tableau chromatiques. *Mem Soc d'anthropol de Paris* ser 1, v. 2: 113–125.

Brues, Alice M. 1977. People and races. New York: Macmillan.

Buettner-Janusch, John. 1973. *Physical anthropology: a perspective.* New York, London, Sydney, Toronto: John Wiley.

Cirlot, J. E. 1962. *A dictionary of symbols.* New York: Philosophical Library.

Clegg, E. J. 1968. The study of man: an introduction to human biology. New York: American Elsevier.

Clements, F. W. 1931. Relation between skin color and degree of tanning. *Am J Phys Anthropol* 483–503.

Cockayne, E. A. 1933. *Inherited abnormalities of the skin and its appendages.* London: Oxford University Press, Humphrey Milford.

Cole, Sonia. 1963. *Races of man.* London: Trustees of the British Museum.

Comas, Juan. 1966. *Manual de antropología física.* Mexico, D.F.: Univ. Nacional Autonómica de Mexico, Instituto de Investigaciones Históricos.

Coon, Carleton S. 1969. *The living races of man.* New York: Alfred A. Knopf.

Coon, Carleton S., Garn, Stanley, Birdsell, Joseph B. 1950. *Races: A study of the problems of race formation in man.* Springfield, Illinois: Charles C Thomas.

Count, Earl W., ed. 1950. *This is race.* New York: Henry Schumann.

Cowles, R. B. 1959. Some ecological factors bearing on the origin and evolution of pigment in the human skin. *Am Naturalist 93:* 283–293.

Cowles, R. B. 1967. Black pigmentation: adaptation for concealment or heat conservation. *Science 158:* 340–1341.

Daniels, Farrington, Jr. 1964. Man and radiant energy: solar radiation. In Dill, D. B., ed. 1964, ch. 62, pp. 969–987.

Darwin, Charles. 1896. *The descent of man and selection in relation to sex.* New York: D. Appleton.

Davenport, Charles B. 1926. The skin colors of the races of mankind. *Nat Hist 26:* 44–49.

Deniker, J. 1900. *The races of man: an outline of anthropology and ethnology.* London: Walter Scott.

Dill, D. B., ed. 1964. *Handbook of physiology, Section 4: Adaptation to the environment.* Washington, D.C.: Amer physiological Soc.

Dobzhansky, Theodosius, Ayala, Francisco J., Stebbins, G. Ledyard, and Valentine, James W. 1977. *Evolution.* San Francisco: W. H. Freeman.

Dubos, René. 1965. *Man adapting.* New Haven and London: Yale Univ. Press.

Duchon, Jiri, Fitzpatrick, Thomas B., and Seiji, Makoto. Melanin 1968: some definitions and problems. In *Yearbook of Dermatology 1967–1968,* pp. 6–33.

Edwards, E. A., and Duntley, S. Q. 1939. The pigments and color of living human skin. *Am J Anat 65:* 1–33.

Fitzpatrick, Thomas B., Wick, Michael M., and Toda, Kyoshi, eds. 1986. *Brown melanoderma: biology and disease of epidermal pigmentation.* Tokyo, Japan: University of Tokyo Press.

Fleure, H. J. 1927. *The characters of the human skin in their relations to questions of race and health.* London: Oxford U. Press, Humphrey Milford.

Fleure, H. J. 1945. The distribution of skin color. *Geographical Rev 35:* 580–595.

Garn, Stanley M. 1961. *Human races.* Springfield, Illinois: Charles C Thomas.

Gates, R. Ruggles. 1946. *Human genetics* (vols. 1 and 2). New York: Macmillan.

Gifford, Sanford R. 1942. *A textbook of ophthalmology.* Philadelphia and London: W. B. Saunders.

Goldsby, Richard A. 1971. *Race and races.* New York: Macmillan.

Gordon, Myron, ed. 1959. *Pigment cell biology: proceedings of the fourth conference on the biology of normal and atypical pigment cell growth.* New York: Academic Press.

Gould, George M., and Pyle, Walter L. 1956. *Anomalies and curiosities of medicine.* New York: Bell. [reprint of 1896 edition]

Hamilton, William J. 1973. *Life's color code.* New York: McGraw-Hill.

Harrison, G. A., Weiner, J. S., Tanner, J. M., and Barnicot, N. A. 1964. *Human biology, and introduction to human evolution, variation and growth.* New York and Oxford: Oxford U. Press.

Henderson, I. F., and Henderson, W. D. 1963. *A dictionary of biological terms.* 8th ed. Ed. by J. H. Henneth. Princeton, New Jersey: D. Van Nostrand.

Hesch, M. 1931. *Über Pigmentierungsverhältnisse des menlischen Iris nach Alter und Geschlecht.* Stuttgart: Verhandlungen der Gesellschaft für Physiche Anthropolgie 5: 9–25.

Hooton, Earnest Albert. 1946. *Up from the ape.* New York: Macmillan.

Hrdlička, Aleš. 1904. Directions for collecting information and specimens for physical anthropology. Part R, Bull U.S. Nat Museum No. 39. Washington, D.C.: Government Printing Office.

Hrdlička, Aleš. 1920 *Anthropometry.* Philadelphia: Wistar Institute of Anatomy and Biology.

Hunter, Donald. 1969. *The diseases of occupations.* London: The English Universities Press.

Jenness, Diamond. 1921. The "blond" Eskimos. *Amer Anthropol 23*(3): 257–267.

King, James C. 1971. *The biology of race.* New York, Chicago, San Francisco, Atlanta: Harcourt, Brace, Jovanovich.

Ladell, William S. S. *Terrestrial animals in humid heat: man.* In Dill, D. B., ed. 1964: 625–659.

Lee, Marjorie M. C., and Lasker, Gabriel W. 1959. The sun-tanning potential of human skin. *Human Biol 31*(3): 252–260.

Lewontin, Richard. 1982. *Human diversity.* New York: Scientific American Books.

Loomis, W. F. 1970. Rickets. *Sci Am 223*(6): 77–91.

Marks, E. 1943. Skin color judgments of Negro college students. *J Abnorm and Soc Psych 38:* 370–376.

Martin, Rudolf, and Saller, Karl. 1956. *Lehrbuch der Anthropologie in systematische Darstellung.* Stuttgart: Gustav Fischer Verlag.

Mather, Kenneth. 1964. *Human diversity: The nature and significance of differences among men.* Edinburgh and London: Oliver and Boyd.

McKusick, Victor A. 1964. *Human genetics.* Englewood Cliffs, New Jersey: Prentice-Hall.

Mitchell, G. A. G., and Patterson, E. L. 1954. *Basic anatomy.* Edinburgh and London: E. & S. Livingstone.

Molnar, Stephen. 1983. *Human variation: races, types and ethnic groups.* 2nd ed. Englewood Cliffs, New Jersey: Prentice-Hall.

Montagu, M. F. Ashley. 1960. *A handbook of anthropometry.* Springfield, Illinois: Charles C Thomas.

Moses, Robert A., ed. 1981. *Adler's physiology of the eye: clinical application.* 7th ed. St. Louis, Toronto, London: C. V. Mosby.

Olivier, Georges. 1965. *Anatomie Anthropologiques.* Paris: Vigot Frères, Éditeurs. pp. 419–447.

Olivier, Georges. 1969. *Practical anthropology.* Springfield, Illinois: Charles C Thomas.

Pales, L. 1932. Premières recherches dur la tache pigmentaire congénitale (Tache mongolique) en Afrique équatoriale francaise. *J Soc des Africanistes 2:* 55–58.

Pathak, Madhu A. Clinical and therapeutic aspects of melasma: an overview. In Fitzpatrick, Wick and Toda 1986: 161–172.

Price, A. Grenfell. 1939. *White settlers in the tropics.* New York: Amer Geog Soc Spec Pub 23.

Razran, G. 1950. Ethnic dislikes and stereotypes. *J Abnorm and Soc Psych 45:* 7–27.

Riley, P. A. 1977. The mechanism of melanogenesis. *Symp Zool Soc Lond 39:* 77–95.

Riley, Vernon, ed. 1972. *Pigmentation: its genesis and biologic control.* New York: Appleton-Century-Crofts.

Rozprým, F. 1934. Eyebrows and eyelids in man: their different forms, pigmentation and heredity. *J Roy Anthrop Inst 64:* 353–395.

Searle, A. G. 1968. *Comparative genetics of coat colour in mammals.* London: Logos Press, Ltd./Elek Press, Limited.

Sheard, C., and Brown, George E. 1926. The spectrophotometric analysis of the color of the skin, and the observations by this method in normal and pathological subjects. *Arch Internal Med 38:* 816–831.

Sohal, R. S., ed. 1981. *Age pigments.* Amsterdam, New York, Oxford: Elsevier; North Holland: Biomedical Press.

Spooner, J. D. 1957. *Ocular anatomy: the anatomy, histology, embryology, ontogeny and phylogeny of the human eye and related structures.* London: Hatton Press.

Stewart, T. D., ed. 1947. *Hrdlička's practical anthropometry.* Philadelphia: The Wistar Institute of Anatomy and Biology.

Sullivan, Louis R. 1928. *Essentials of anthropometry: a handbook for explorers and museum collectors.* New York: Amer Museum of Nat Hist.

Szabó, George. 1959. Quantitative histological investigation of the melanocyte system of the human epidermis. In Gordon 1959: 99–125.

Taussig, J., and Williams, G. D. 1940. Skin color and skin cancer. *Arch Pathol 30:* 721–730.

Todd, T. Wingate, Blackwood, Beatrice, and Beecher, Harry. 1928. Skin pigmentation: the color top method of recording. *Am J Phys Anthropol 11*(2): 187–204.

Ubelaker, Douglas H. 1989. *Human skeletal remains: excavation, analysis, interpretation.* 2nd ed. Washington, D.C.: Teraxcum Washington.

Washburn, S. L. 1963. The study of race. *Am Anthropol 65:* 521–531.

Washburn, S. L. 1964. Racial differences in skin color. *Am Anthropol 66:* 1173–1174.

Wassermann, H. P. 1974. *Ethnic pigmentation: historical, physiological and clinical aspects.* Amsterdam: Excerpta Medica.

Weiner, J. S. 1951. A spectrophotometer for measurement of skin color. *Man 51*(253): 152–153.

Weniger, Josef. 1954. Variabilität der Structur der Menlischer Iris. *Homo 5*(2–4): 135–148.

Williams, Peter L., and Warwick, Roger. 1980. *Gray's anatomy.* Philadelphia: W. B. Saunders.

Wolman, Moshe, ed. 1969. *Pigments in pathology.* New York and London: Academic Press.

Young, J. Z. 1971. An introduction to the study of man. Oxford: Clarendon Press.

GLOSSARY

ACTINIC. Radiation by which chemical effects are produced.

ADDISON'S DISEASE. A disease caused by the underfunctioning of the adrenal glands that involves darkening of the skin and the membranes of the mouth.

ALBINISM, ALBINOISM. A condition caused by a deficiency from birth of normal pigmentation of the skin, hair, and iris of the eyes.

APOSEMATIC. Having colors or markings that frighten away enemies.

ARCUS JUVENILIS. A ring around the corneal margin of the iris of the eye that may occur congenitally in children.

ARCUS SINILIS. A white ring around the margin of the cornea of the eye resulting from a fatty degeneration of the corneal tissue, usually occurring in persons 50 years of age and older.

CAROTENE. The orange or red pigment that occurs in carrots, sweet potatoes, and other vegetables, also milk fat and egg yolk. It can be converted into vitamin A in the body.

CAUCASOID, MONGOLOID, NEGROID. Terms of racial classification based on a number of anatomic details including skin color.

CORIUM. The skin layer under the epidermis, the true skin or dermis.

CORNEA. The transparent covering of the front portion of the eyeball. Through pathological conditions it may become more or less opaque, which destroys acuity of vision.

CRYPTIC COLORATION. A concealing color scheme that makes its possessor resemble its background.

CYANOSIS. A bluish, greyish or dark purple discoloration of the skin resulting from deficient oxygenation of the blood.

DISRUPTIVE COLORATION. A color scheme using contrasting colors to distract attention from the true outlines of an animal or object.

ERYTHEMA. A diffused redness of the skin resulting from congestion of the capillaries.

GOLGER'S RULE. The principle that animals and birds that live in the wet tropics are dark in color but those that dwell in or near the Arctic tend to be light colored.

HEMOGLOBIN. An oxygen bearing red pigment in the blood cells composed of the iron carrying pigment *heme* linked to the protein *globin*. It transports oxygen within the body.

HETEROCHROMIA IRIDIS. Different color of the iris of the two eyes.

53

IRIS. The colored muscular diaphragm in front of the lens of the eye. It regulates the amount of light entering the eye and gives color to the eye.

LEUCODERM. White skin: a term of primary racial classification including those peoples of light or "white" skin.

MACULE or MACULA. A stain or discolored spot in the skin not elevated above the surface. Also a dense condition of the cornea that obscures vision.

MELANIN. A dark brown to black sulfur-containing pigment that occurs in the skin, hair, and choroid layer and iris of the eyes. It exists in certain tumors known as melanomas.

MELANOCYTE. A cell of the epidermis that synthesizes melanin.

MELANODERM. A term of primary racial classification for peoples of dark skin.

MELANOSOME. The pigment granule produced by melanocytes.

MELASMA. An acquired excessive deposition of brown or greyish brown pigments in the face, neck, and occasionally forearm.

MONGOLIAN SPOT, also BLUE SPOT. A dark bluish or mulberry colored round or oval spot usually in the sacral region, present from birth.

MUTATION. An alteration in a gene that produces a change in later generations of an organism; not caused by normal genetic processes.

OXYHEMOGLOBIN. The bright red pigmentation resulting from a combination of hemoglobin with oxygen. Oxyhemoglobin transports oxygen from the lungs to the various body tissues.

PHENOCOPY. The result of an environmentally induced condition that resembles the expression of a known genetic mutation.

PIEBALD SKIN. Skin having patches of color or patches without pigmentation.

PINTA. A treponemal disease occurring in the hot lowlands of the Americas characterized by red to deep blue papules on the skin.

RETINA. The light sensitive layer that lines the interior surface of the eyeball. It contains the rods and cones and pigment cells.

SCATTERING. An optical effect when a beam of light passes from one medium to another and particles collide that causes an increased intensity of the blue end of the spectrum and diminished redness.

SCLERA or SCLEROTIC COAT. The tough white fibrous outer layer of the eyeball.

SPECTROPHOTOMETER. An instrument for measuring the wavelengths of the components of reflected light.

STRATUM CORNEUM. The outermost or horny layer of the skin.

STRATUM GERMINATIVUM. The lowest layers of the epidermis from which the other layers are derived; also called the *malpighian layer*.

STRATUM GRANULOSUM. A thin layer of the epidermis most clearly observable in the thickened skin of the palm of the hand and the sole of the foot.

STRATUM LUCIDUM. A thin layer of translucent cells of the epidermis between the stratum corneum and the stratum granulosum.

TYROSINE. A crystalline amino acid that is converted in the body into the brown pigment melanin.

VITILIGO. A condition of unknown cause resulting from defective melanin formation in the skin and characterized by sharply demarkated milky white patches.

XANTHODERM. Yellow skin: a term used for a primary racial group of yellow to brown skin color.

NAME INDEX

57

SUBJECT INDEX

A

Addison's disease, 32
Albinism, 25
Arcus juvenalis, 19
Arcus senilis, 19
Atabrine (a brand of quinacrine), 32

B

Blood, influence of, on skin color, 7
Blood types, 23

C

Camouflage, role of skin color in, 43
Canities, 30
Canthexalin, 32
Carotene, 5, 22
Chlorosis, 31
Climate, effect of, on pigmentation, 23
Color top, 8, 9
Contact dermatitis, 31
Core temperature, 43
Cyanosis, 30

E

Egyptians, 22, 33
Ephelides (*see* Freckling)
Erythema, 31
Eye, color classification of, 18, 19
Eye color, heredity of, 19
Eyes, structure of, 16, 17

F

Freckling, 12, 29

H

Hair, color of, 14, 15
Hair, functions of, 12, 13
Hair, greying of, 15, 16
Hair, structure of, 13, 14
Hemoglobin, 5, 22

I

Icteris (*see* Jaundice)

J

Jaundice, 34

L

Lentigo, 29
Leukotrichia, 30
Leukodermia (*see* Vitiligo)

M

Melanin, 4, 5, 6
Melanocytes, 4, 6
Melanoid, 4
Melanosomes, 4
Melasma, 32
Mongolian spot, 29
Mutations, 24

N

Nevus flammeus, 30

O

Osteomalacia (*see* Rickets)
Oxyhemoglobin, 5, 13

59